Who Was Johnny Cash?

by Jim Gigliotti

illustrated by Gregory Copeland

Penguin Workshop

For Gracie and Jeff, may your love grow as
legendary as Johnny and June's—JG

To a wonderful man and friend, Souch—GC

PENGUIN WORKSHOP
An imprint of Penguin Random House LLC, New York

First published in the United States of America by Penguin Workshop,
an imprint of Penguin Random House LLC, New York, 2022

Text copyright © 2022 by Jim E. Gigliotti
Illustrations copyright © 2022 by Penguin Random House LLC

Visit us online at penguinrandomhouse.com.

Library of Congress Cataloging-in-Publication Data is available.

Printed in the United States of America

ISBN 9780399544163 (paperback)   10 9 8 7 6 5 4 3 2 1 WOR
ISBN 9780399544187 (library binding)   10 9 8 7 6 5 4 3 2 1 WOR

Contents

Who Was Johnny Cash?

J.R. Cash burst through the back door of the family's house in Dyess, Arkansas, one day in 1947. As usual, he was singing.

J.R. was fifteen years old at the time. His mom, Carrie, was at the kitchen stove. She had her back to him. "Who was that?" she said.

Carrie knew perfectly well who it was. She had heard J.R. singing along with his brothers and sisters many times before while the entire family picked cotton during long, hot days in the fields. But she also knew that on this day something was

different. J.R.'s voice was deeper. It was richer. It was stronger. This was a voice she had not heard before.

J.R.'s voice was changing. Like many teenage boys, J.R.'s voice was beginning to sound different. "You sound exactly like my daddy," Carrie said. Her father, J.R.'s grandfather, had been known for many miles around for his singing.

Carrie told J.R. his voice was a gift. "God has his hand on you, son," she said. "Don't ever forget the gift." That voice was indeed a gift, and it would help him build a long and successful music career. J.R. would grow up to be known as Johnny Cash, and go on to sell more than ninety million albums around the world.

Johnny's music is most often considered country, which is sometimes called country and western. But he also sang many other different types of music, including songs that featured the sounds of gospel, blues, folk, and rock.

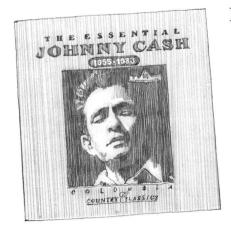

He appealed to so many different music fans that he has been inducted into the Country Music Hall of Fame, the Rock and Roll Hall of Fame, and the Gospel Music Hall of Fame.

And he never forgot that his voice was a gift. He used it to speak out, in words and in song, on behalf of Native Americans, poor people, prison inmates, and others.

Johnny saw the struggles of people and wanted to help. Maybe that's because he had so many of his own struggles over the years. He had grown up in a poor family in rural Arkansas. And even after he became famous, he worked to overcome a personal battle with drugs to build a lasting career. Many of Johnny's most famous songs are about the themes of struggle, recovery, and overcoming hardship.

His appeal to many different audiences, his commitment to social justice, and his dedication to using his gift to help others made Johnny Cash one of the most important artists in music history.

CHAPTER 1
The Promised Land

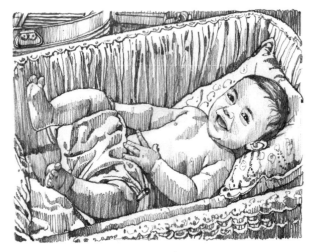

J.R. Cash

Johnny Cash was born on February 26, 1932, in Kingsland, Arkansas, a small town of only several hundred people. His mother, Carrie, wanted to name him John. His father, Ray, wanted to name him Ray. When they couldn't agree, they settled on simply the initials

"J.R." Johnny was called J.R. throughout his childhood.

Johnny was the fourth of Carrie and Ray's seven children. He had two older brothers, Roy and Jack, and an older sister, Louise. Two more girls, Reba and Joanne, and another boy, Tommy, came later.

The Cash family

The United States was in the midst of the Great Depression when Johnny was born. Many people were out of work. Life was difficult, including at the Cash house. In Kingsland, Johnny's dad did whatever work he could find wherever he could find it. That might mean walking several miles in the morning to pick crops or to work construction jobs, then walking several miles back in the evening with $1.50 or so to show for a full day's work.

Johnny's father, Ray

Carrie did the best she could, but raising a family at that time was not easy. The house had no indoor running water or electricity. It didn't even have windows! To keep out the winter weather, Carrie would hang blankets or burlap sacks over the open spaces where windows should have been. The entire house shook whenever a train went by on the nearby railroad tracks.

Johnny was still a toddler when his father heard a report on the radio about the government building a new community that would be called Dyess (say: DIE-iss), Arkansas, about two hundred miles northeast of Kingsland. Ray jumped at the chance to apply to live there. He joined thousands of other applicants in Arkansas. The Cash family was one of about six hundred families selected to participate in a program that was part of the US government's New Deal.

Each family that was in the Work Projects Administration program received at least twenty acres of land with a house and a barn. They also received a mule to help them work the land, and enough money to get them going on the first year's crops.

The families had to pay back the government with money they earned from selling those crops. And before they could plant anything, they had to clear the land and make it suitable for farming. Doing that would take a lot of hard work.

And so, one day in March 1935, Ray and Carrie Cash, and their five children at the time, including three-year-old Johnny, squeezed into a flatbed truck along with everything they owned, which wasn't much.

The Great Depression and the New Deal

The Great Depression was an extended time of financial hardship in the United States and around the world from 1929 to 1939. It began when the US stock market crashed—meaning stocks dropped significantly in price—on October 24, 1929.

During the Great Depression, many Americans lost their jobs. About one out of every four adult Americans was out of work in the mid-1930s. That made it difficult or impossible for them to pay for their homes, or to buy groceries. Many even lost their life savings in the stock market.

To combat the Great Depression, US president Franklin D. Roosevelt began a series of programs in the 1930s called the New Deal. They provided help for many people, especially farmers and the unemployed, by establishing public works projects (like building Dyess), reforming the banking industry, and establishing the Social Security Administration to help ensure that American citizens could count on some basic benefits.

President Franklin D. Roosevelt

Johnny rode with Roy and Jack in the open back end of the truck. His mother rode with Louise and one-year-old Reba up front with his dad. Over two long days, the boys bumped up and down in the back as the truck drove over potholes in the muddy roads toward Dyess. At

night, they tried to sleep under the cover of a tarp that protected them from the bitter cold and rain.

To pass the time and keep her children calm, Carrie sang gospel hymns such as "I Am Bound for the Promised Land." That's the first song Johnny remembered hearing *ever*. And, he said many years later, it really was like they were bound for the promised land.

What the Cashes found in Dyess seemed simply amazing. Instead of blankets covering the window openings, like their house in Kingsland had, the house had glass windows. Instead of old peeling paint, the house in Dyess had a fresh coat of white paint with a green-shingled roof. And instead of land tired and worn from planting crops year after year, it had rich and fertile soil.

The Dyess house had no electricity or running water, but for the Cash family, it seemed like heaven. It had "luxuries untold," Johnny would later write, including two bedrooms for the family members to sleep in, a front porch and a back porch, and an outside toilet, called an outhouse.

The Cash family's Arkansas home

Still, there was much work to be done. The fields surrounding the house were overgrown with trees and weeds and vines, tangled and thick.

They all had to be cleared before the first crops could be planted.

Johnny's father and oldest brother, Roy, worked from dawn until dusk six days a week. They cleared three acres that first spring and planted their first cottonseeds. By the following spring, a large cotton crop helped the family start paying back the US government for its new home.

CHAPTER 2
Radio Dreams

Not long after the Cash family moved to Dyess, a large package arrived in the mail. Ray Cash had bought a radio from the Sears, Roebuck catalog!

Because there was no electricity in the house, the radio was powered by a big battery. Listening to the new radio was the only way young Johnny could hear gospel and other music he didn't already know from singing with his family and friends.

The first song Johnny remembered hearing on the radio was "Hobo Bill's Last Ride," by country music star Jimmie Rodgers. He was hooked. "From that day on, I wanted to sing on the radio," he said.

When Johnny was five, he began working in the cotton fields as a water boy. He would bring water to his mom and dad and older siblings as they worked under the hot Arkansas sun. When he was eight, he started picking cotton. He would fill a bag with thirty pounds of cotton, drag it over to load onto a wagon, then start over again—as many as seven, eight, or nine times a day. When he was a little older, the sack grew to be a forty- or fifty-pound bag. Sometimes, Johnny would have to miss school to work the fields. After all, the family needed to sell enough cotton to buy groceries and pay its bills.

Each night, just after the evening news ended at 8:05, Johnny's father would go to bed. He had to get up early the next morning to work the fields. "Turn that radio off!" Ray would yell.

Johnny would turn the sound down as low as he could and press his ear right up against the speaker. He would listen to country songs by Jimmie Rodgers and Gene Autry, gospel songs by Sister Rosetta Tharpe, and folk music by the Carter  Family. "The music I heard became the best thing in my life," he wrote many years later.

Johnny's deep interest in music didn't sit well with Ray. He thought Johnny should be doing more useful things than sitting in front of the radio. "You're wasting your time listening to them old records on the radio," Ray would say. "That's going to keep you from making a living. You'll never do any good as long as you've got that music on the mind."

Jimmie Rodgers (1897–1933)

Jimmie Rodgers is sometimes called the father of country music. He brought a unique style, humor, and a distinctive yodel to his music.

Rodgers was born near Meridian, Mississippi, in 1897. He quit school at age fourteen and worked various jobs, including as a brakeman on a railroad line, which is where he learned to play the guitar and banjo and picked up a wide range of musical styles. His nickname was "the Singing Brakeman."

He began playing on a local radio station in Asheville, North Carolina, in 1927. The next year, he recorded his first big hit, "Blue Yodel," sometimes called "T for Texas." Various versions of the single sold nearly five hundred thousand copies by the end of the decade, making Rodgers a star. Over the next several years, he went on to make more than one hundred records that helped shape the future of country music. Many country stars have been influenced by his sound.

Rodgers was only thirty-five when he died in 1933 from the effects of tuberculosis. He was one of the original inductees of the Country Music Hall of Fame in 1961. But he had such a huge impact on music history that he is also a member of the Rock and Roll Hall of Fame, the Blues Hall of Fame, and the Songwriters Hall of Fame.

The Carter Family

The husband-and-wife trio of A.P. and Sara Carter and his sister-in-law Maybelle Carter formed the original members of the Carter Family. They sang together informally before making their first recording in 1927 for a talent scout for Victor

Records. Over the next three years, their records sold three hundred thousand copies.

The Carter Family helped popularize American folk music and eventually recorded more than three hundred songs. The trio's harmonizing style and guitar picking also influenced country music. Some of their best-known songs include "Keep on the Sunny Side," "Wabash Cannonball," and "Wildwood Flower."

Around 1940, A.P. and Sara's children, Janette and Joe Carter, joined the group. So did Maybelle's daughters, Helen, June, and Anita Carter. After the group disbanded in 1944, Maybelle continued to perform with her daughters, often as the Carter Sisters and Mother Maybelle. A.P., Sara, and their children performed as the A.P. Carter Family.

The Carter Family was inducted into the Country Music Hall of Fame in 1970, and into the Grammy Hall of Fame in 1988.

Johnny's mother, on the other hand, was happy about her son's interest in music. From her, Johnny learned many of the gospel songs that he loved for the rest of his life. "What would you give," Carrie would begin singing, and Johnny would

finish the line with, "in exchange for your soul?"

The two sang everywhere—in the house, on the porch, out in the fields, and at Dyess Baptist Church, which they would attend three days a week. Carrie played the guitar and the fiddle.

Her father had been a gifted singer who, according to Johnny, people came from all over the county to listen to. "Mama saw that the music was in me just as it was in her and had been in her father," Johnny said. He told her how he wanted to be on the radio one day, and she encouraged him.

Jack Cash

Of all his siblings, Johnny was closest to his brother Jack, who was two years older. Twelve-year-old Johnny was devastated, then, when Jack died in 1944, after he was injured by a table saw.

The loss was terrible for the entire family, but it struck Johnny especially hard. "Jack was my big brother and my hero," Johnny wrote many years later. "My best friend, my big buddy, my mentor, and my protector."

The morning of the funeral, Johnny got up early, found a shovel, and helped dig Jack's grave. He went to church muddy and dirty from the effort, and without shoes. He couldn't put them on because he'd injured his foot stepping on a nail. But he didn't care. His best friend was gone.

For the rest of his life, Johnny dreamed of his brother. And for the rest of his life, whenever Johnny found himself not knowing what to do in a situation, he searched for the answer by thinking, *What would Jack do?*

Johnny was sad for a long time without his brother and best friend. But in 1945, about a year after Jack's death, he made a new friend. His name was Pete Barnhill. He had polio, a disease that made it difficult to walk and left him without the use of one of his arms. But Pete didn't let polio stop him from learning to play the guitar. Johnny would go to his house every day after school. Pete tried to teach Johnny to play guitar, but Johnny wasn't very good at it. So the two of them would sing the country songs that were popular at the time by artists such as Hank Snow, Ernest Tubb, and Jimmie Rodgers.

It would be long past sundown by the time

Johnny would walk back home from Pete's house. It was scary walking in the dark, but Johnny kept his fear away by singing.

Mrs. Ruby Cooley taught Johnny math for several years in grade school and high school. "He was an excellent student," she said. "But that wasn't all he was." He was also the school's star performer. Every year, the school would perform a play. "Which part is J.R. going to play?" the kids would ask. "After he'd chosen his part, then the other kids would try out," Mrs. Cooley recalled.

Johnny was a class vice president his senior year at Dyess High School, and he sang at graduation there in 1950. His grades were good, but college was "almost unattainable for a cotton-farm boy," Johnny later recalled. He still wanted to be a musician, but he didn't know how to get started. So he began looking for a job. He tried strawberry picking in Arkansas. But the harvests were so small, they lasted only three days. He tried working on an assembly line at an automobile factory in Michigan. He then tried working at a margarine plant near Dyess. But the work was dirty and smelly, so he quit after only a few days.

In 1950, eighteen-year-old Johnny decided to join the US Air Force. At the time, he was still called J.R. But the man at the Air Force recruiting office wouldn't accept initials (Johnny's real name was simply J.R. after all) on the application. So J.R. listed John, the name his mother had wanted to give him at birth, as

Johnny in his Air Force uniform

his first name. He was now John Cash.

In San Antonio, Texas, Johnny did so well during basic training for the Air Force that he had his pick of jobs. He chose radio operator because, well, it sounded like it had something to do with radios! It didn't, at least not in the sense of the radio he used to listen to back home in Dyess.

Johnny's job wasn't to broadcast anything over the radio but to listen to messages sent in Morse code and transcribe them for the Air Force.

He was given his choice of where to work: a US Air Force base in Alaska, or one in Germany. He chose Germany because he wanted to see Europe.

CHAPTER 3
In Love

Before Johnny left for Germany, he remained at the Air Force base in San Antonio, Texas, to receive special training for his job as a radio operator. He had been in San Antonio almost three months when he and a fellow soldier went to a local roller-skating rink.

There, Johnny noticed the prettiest girl he had ever seen. Her name was Vivian Liberto. She was seventeen, and had dark hair and beautiful, hazel-colored eyes. Johnny liked her right away. "Would you like to skate with me?" he asked.

They skated until closing time, and then she let Johnny take her home on the bus. However, she wouldn't let him kiss her—not on the first date!

Over the next three weeks, Johnny and Vivian saw as much of each other as his Air Force schedule allowed. They went to the movies and out for ice cream. He met her parents, and her older brother and younger sister. Three weeks wasn't a long time,

but it was enough to know they wanted to get to know each other even better. Johnny promised to write every day from Germany.

After a short trip back home to Dyess and a stop in New York City, Johnny boarded the USNS *General W. G. Haan*, in Brooklyn, New York, on September 20, 1951. He was on his way to Landsberg Air Force Base in Germany.

There, it turned out that Johnny was very good at transcribing Morse code. In fact, he was the best man at it on the base. Maybe that's not surprising. After all, it was already apparent that he had a great ear for music. Listening in to the communications over his radio equipment and figuring out what the dots and dashes of Morse code meant took a great ear, too.

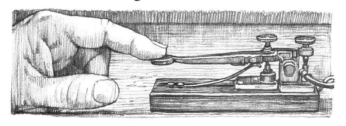

Morse telegraph key

One added benefit to working with radio equipment was that on Sunday mornings, Johnny could have his receiver pick up radio station WSM all the way back in Nashville, Tennessee. Because of the time difference, it was Saturday night in the United States. So Johnny listened to the *Grand Ole Opry* on WSM, just like he would have been doing back home. He still dreamed of being one of those singers on the radio one day.

While at Landsberg, Johnny bought his first guitar for twenty German deutsche marks—about five US dollars at the time. Johnny remembered the day he bought his guitar well. That's because he had to carry it four miles through the snow to get back to the Air Force base! "I was numb all over," he said.

It was worth it because Johnny taught himself to play. One cold, rainy morning, he sat in the barracks with his guitar and wrote a song called

"Wide Open Road." He also wrote a poem called "Hey, Porter." At the base in 1951, Johnny watched the movie *Inside the Walls of Folsom Prison*, about men in jail who riot over how badly they are treated by prison guards. That movie inspired him to write a song called "Folsom Prison Blues." The movie was not a true story. But it made Johnny think about how awful life inside a prison could be.

Grand Ole Opry

Being asked to perform on the *Grand Ole Opry*, also known as Country Music's Most Famous Stage, is one of the top honors a country music artist can receive.

The *Grand Ole Opry* is a weekly radio show that airs on Nashville station WSM on Saturday nights. The show began in 1925, when it was first called *WSM Barn Dance*, making it the longest-running radio show in US history. In addition to music by country stars past and present, the *Grand Ole Opry* includes comedy acts and skits. From 1943 to 1974, it was broadcast from the Ryman Auditorium in downtown Nashville.

Country music's biggest stars have performed at "the opry"—a casual way of saying "opera"—over the years, including Bob Wills, Roy Acuff, the Carter Family, Patsy Cline, Willie Nelson, Loretta Lynn, and Dolly Parton.

Today, fans not in range of WSM can listen in on satellite radio or streaming on the station's website.

A couple of other men in Johnny's unit in Germany also played the guitar. Another played the mandolin. They all began playing together, calling themselves the Landsberg Barbarians. Their versions of the country songs they heard on the radio and the gospel songs they remembered from their youth weren't very good. However, just playing those songs made Johnny feel closer to home.

When Johnny wasn't working or playing with the Landsberg Barbarians, he kept his promise

and wrote to Vivian every day. Sometimes, it was two or three times in a single day! Even though Johnny was in Germany for less than three years, he and Vivian exchanged more than a thousand letters. In one of his letters, Johnny told Vivian about his dreams of being on the radio. In one of her letters, Vivian included a photo of herself. Johnny tacked it to

the wall above his bunk. It was the last thing he saw at night before he went to sleep and the first thing he saw when he woke up in the morning. Johnny and Vivian decided they were going to marry someday soon after he got out of the service.

That day came in 1954. The Air Force had given Johnny a promotion and wanted him to stay on longer. But Johnny decided that he was going back to the United States to get married and pursue his singing career. He was honorably discharged and left Germany on July 3. Just five weeks later, on August 7, he and Vivian were married by her uncle, a priest, at a Roman Catholic church in San Antonio.

CHAPTER 4
On His Way

After they married in 1954, Johnny and Vivian moved to Memphis, Tennessee, where Johnny's older brother, Roy, lived. Roy was a mechanic but also wanted to be a musician. At the time, there were few places in the United States better than Memphis for breaking into the music business.

Memphis was a home base to a wide range of music, including country, gospel, blues, rock and roll, and an emerging sound that would come to be known as rockabilly—a combination of country and rock and roll.

To help make ends meet in Memphis, Johnny took a job selling kitchen appliances.

He tried hard, but his heart just wasn't in it. His focus was always on music.

One day, Roy Cash suggested that Johnny stop by the car dealership where he worked. A couple of the mechanics there were musicians, and Roy thought Johnny should meet them.

So Johnny did, and he and Luther Perkins and Marshall Grant hit it off. They soon began meeting after work. Their wives became friends, too, and would cook and chat while their husbands practiced.

The trouble was, all three played pretty much the same sound on a rhythm guitar. They realized that if they were ever going to be on the radio, they would have to do something different to make their sound unique.

"Well, since I do most of the singing, maybe

I should stick with this rhythm guitar," Johnny said.

"I know where I can borrow an electric guitar," Perkins said.

That left the need for a bass, which they also borrowed and which Grant volunteered to play.

Johnny plays a rhythm guitar, Perkins plays an electric guitar, and Grant plays a bass

Perkins and Grant were not skilled musicians at the time. They played simply and methodically—almost like typing on a keyboard one letter at a time. However, their inexperience gave them an advantage. It created an entirely different sound. Music critics and performers, including Johnny, came to describe the sound as "boom-chicka-boom." It didn't sound like anything else in country music. And it was about to help fulfill Johnny's dream of singing on the radio.

One day in November 1954, Johnny headed to the office of the Sun Record Company, also known as Sun Records. It was the record company in Memphis that had recently signed Elvis Presley. Johnny had gotten up early, grabbed his guitar, and went to Sun. He sat on the front steps and waited until Sam Phillips arrived for work.

"Right off, I was drawn to [his] voice," Phillips said of Johnny's voice. It was unlike any Phillips had ever heard.

Sam Phillips

Phillips told Johnny to come back the next day—but, this time, to bring musicians with him. Then, after meeting Luther Perkins and Marshall Grant, he told them all to come back with a song he could record.

Johnny remembered the poem he wrote in the Air Force barracks in Germany. "Hey, Porter" is about a man riding a train to his home in Tennessee. The man gets more and more excited

as the train gets closer to his home. Johnny turned the poem into a song. Phillips loved it. He thought it could be a hit.

"Hey, Porter" was released on June 21, 1955. Phillips thought *John Cash* sounded a little too old

for the teenagers and young adults who bought most of his records. He wanted his new recording artist to be known as *Johnny*. Luther Perkins and Marshall Grant became the Tennessee Two—even though neither of them was from Tennessee!

Sun Records

Sun Records was a record company that was founded by Sam Phillips in Memphis, Tennessee, in 1952. The company was the first to produce records for some of the biggest names in music, including Elvis Presley, Charlie Rich, Carl Perkins, Johnny Cash, and Jerry Lee Lewis.

Sun's first national hit was "Bear Cat," by Rufus Thomas Jr., in 1953. One year later, "That's All Right" made nineteen-year-old Elvis Presley a star. Elvis's rockabilly sound combined elements of country, rock and roll, and rhythm and blues.

One morning in December 1956, Carl Perkins, who had recorded the 1955 hit song "Blue Suede

Shoes," went to the Sun Records studio to work on some new material. Phillips asked Jerry Lee Lewis to play piano. Eventually, they were joined by Johnny Cash and Elvis Presley. Johnny, Elvis, Carl, and Jerry Lee sang some of their favorite gospel and country songs together. An article in a Memphis newspaper the day after the unplanned recording session called the foursome the Million Dollar Quartet. The album of the seventeen songs recorded that day was not released until 1981.

The Million Dollar Quartet

Family would still call Johnny *J.R.*, and some close friends would call him *John*. But to the rest of the world, he would always be known as *Johnny Cash*.

Not long after recording "Hey, Porter," Johnny got his first royalty check—his payment based on the record's sales. It was for only $6.42, but, Johnny said, "to me it was like a million dollars." He was on his way to fulfilling his dream of singing on the radio.

"Hey, Porter" reached number fourteen on *Billboard* magazine's country music chart. (*Billboard* publishes weekly listings of the most popular songs and albums in the United States.)

Landing a song on the chart helped Johnny get several small concert dates in Arkansas. Sam Phillips had encouraged him to perform to get more comfortable in front of a live audience. Then, in August 1955, Johnny was asked to play on a brief tour with the wildly popular Elvis Presley in three Southern states.

Soon after "Hey, Porter" began playing on the radio, Johnny recorded "Folsom Prison Blues." It was another hit, reaching as high as number four on the country chart.

Then he wrote one of the songs he would become most famous for: "I Walk the Line," released on May 1, 1956, spent forty-three weeks on the country chart, rising as high as number two. Johnny was becoming a star.

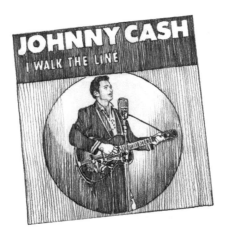

CHAPTER 5
Making a Connection

Johnny wrote "I Walk the Line" to assure his wife, Vivian, that he missed her and would remain faithful to her even when he spent nights performing away from home.

The trouble was, he was away from home more and more. He played 139 concerts in 1957, 116 in 1958, and 101 in 1959. Johnny was getting really popular. But the touring and performing was almost nonstop. One night, for instance, Johnny might have a concert in Little Rock, Arkansas. After the show, he and Marshall and Luther would squeeze themselves and their equipment—including the guitars and a big bass—into Marshall's car and drive through the night to Monroe, Louisiana,

about 175 miles away. They would perform in Monroe, then drive more than 350 miles to Sheffield, Alabama, to perform the next night.

As the lead singer and man out front for the band, Johnny also had to be upbeat and fresh for each performance. There were also the

interviews with radio personalities or newspaper reporters in every town where the band performed. In addition, he dealt with the fans who would come backstage before and after every show to meet him. The demands on his time were exhausting.

To keep up with his schedule and stay on top of his game, Johnny started taking drugs to boost his energy and feel good. At first, it was just one or two pills at a time. But Johnny quickly learned that taking any drugs is a bad idea.

Soon, just one or two pills didn't make him feel so great anymore. Eventually, he was taking pills by the dozens. And yet, it was still never enough.

The drugs started to come between Johnny and Vivian, Johnny and his family, Johnny and God. About the only thing they weren't coming between was Johnny and his music. On July 7, 1956, he made his first appearance on the *Grand Ole Opry* in Nashville, which is where he met June Carter, one of the Carter Family singers, for the first time.

In 1957, he began making regular appearances as a musical guest on television variety shows. And in July 1958, he left Sun Records to join Columbia Records, which promised to let him record the gospel music he still loved so much.

June Carter

Joining Columbia Records meant more money, too. Johnny could afford a new car—

with air-conditioning! He and Vivian and their two young daughters, Rosanne and Kathy, moved that summer to California, where they bought a large house close to Hollywood. He started to act in movies and television shows.

Johnny may have left the South, but the South never left him. Many of his songs came from his own experiences there. "Five Feet High and Rising" told the story of the Tyronza River, which ran right through Dyess. The river overflowed its banks when Johnny was just five years old. It flooded the countryside, including the Cash family farm.

"How high's the water, mama?" the song begins. The water level rises from two feet at the start of the song to three feet, then four, and finally to five. It was at that point in real life that Ray Cash sent the rest of the family back to Kingsland to stay with relatives until the water level went back down.

In early October 1959, Johnny performed on the opening night of the Texas Prison Rodeo in Huntsville. For four days at the annual rodeo, prison inmates competed in various events and were entertained by music and television stars.

Prison inmates compete in a Texas Prison Rodeo event

That year, it rained on opening night. It rained a lot. A thunderstorm knocked out the power onstage. But the inmates didn't want Johnny to go, and he didn't want to leave. So he kept playing. When he sang "Folsom Prison Blues," with no microphone, the inmates crowded the stage so they could hear better. They whooped and hollered, cheered, and asked Johnny to sing it again. So he did.

Johnny had never connected quite like that with any crowd. He was so excited by the reaction that he asked his manager to book another prison concert. Less than three months later, on New Year's Day in 1960, he performed at San Quentin State Prison in California.

Why did Johnny make such a connection with prison audiences? Some of that connection had to do with his image. Johnny's music made him seem like a rebel. He often sang about being in trouble with the law. Some of the prisoners may have believed Johnny had spent time in prison. They weren't alone. Many of Johnny's fans believed the same thing. The truth was that

although Johnny had spent a night in a city jail on several occasions, he had never spent time in prison.

One night in Georgia, Sheriff Ralph Jones put Johnny in a jail cell when he was acting strangely because of the pills he took. The next morning, Sheriff Jones sent him on his way. But first, he had a few words to say.

Sheriff Ralph Jones and Johnny

"Johnny, I would like to understand why you would let a little thing [like] a pill throw you in the gutter and ruin your life," the sheriff said. "Take your pills back and go. Just remember that there are people like us that care for you. And remember, you're a better man than that."

Johnny never forgot those words. And he never forgot to pay that care and concern forward to the inmates he visited during his prison concerts. "We came because we care," one inmate remembered Johnny once telling his prison audience. "We care. We really do. If there's ever anything I can do for you all, let me know somehow, and I'll do it."

Johnny cared about prison reform at a time when that was not a popular idea. He believed the prison system needed to be changed to help inmates, not punish them.

Johnny also cared enough about the treatment of Native Americans to release an entire album  of songs called *Bitter Tears: Ballads of the American Indian* in 1964. The songs are about some of the difficulties Native Americans have faced since the founding of the United States. One of them, "The Ballad of Ira Hayes," tells the true story of a Pima man, Ira Hamilton Hayes, who participated in the famous battle of Iwo Jima during World War II. Many radio stations did not want to play it at first because they thought the subject was too controversial. But "The Ballad of Ira Hayes" eventually rose to number three on *Billboard*'s country chart.

CHAPTER 6
On Top

By the mid-1960s, things were going really well for Johnny in his music career. *Bitter Tears* was his nineteenth album. Two others—*Ring of Fire: The Best of Johnny Cash* and *I Walk the Line*—had reached number one on *Billboard*'s country chart. And "The Ballad of Ira Hayes" was his twenty-fourth *Billboard* top-ten country single!

However, things weren't going well for Johnny at home. He and Vivian had two more daughters, Cindy and Tara. But the girls didn't see their father much. Most of the time, Johnny was away on the road, playing live concerts. When he was home, he was distracted, mostly by the pills he took. Johnny and Vivian's marriage ended in divorce in 1967.

It was June Carter who helped Johnny overcome his addiction to drugs. A country and folk singer since she was ten, June joined Johnny's touring group in the early 1960s and helped write "Ring of Fire," which became Johnny's biggest hit ever. It spent seven weeks at number one on *Billboard*'s country chart in 1963.

June almost left Johnny's tour when she discovered his habit of taking drugs, but he begged her to stay. Eventually, she threw away all his pills. She got him help from a doctor. Then she took care of him while his body fought the effects of withdrawing from the drugs.

Johnny and June fell in love. One day in February 1968, they sang a duet called "Jackson" onstage in London, Ontario, Canada. "Jackson" was a big hit that became the most popular of many duets Johnny and June sang together.

Usually, Johnny would launch into another song after he and June sang "Jackson." But on this night, Johnny stopped the show and stepped up to the microphone.

He turned to June. "Will you marry me?" he asked.

Was this just part of the act? Or was Johnny serious? The seven thousand spectators in the audience didn't know what to think. Neither did June. "Go on, sing another," June stammered.

But Johnny was totally serious. "I'm not gonna sing until you answer me," Johnny said. "Will you marry me?"

June stalled for time. She tried to get the band members to start playing something, but they were as surprised as everyone else. They just stood there. Johnny asked again. Finally, she said, "Yes."

"Okay," Johnny said. "Next song."

One week later, on February 29, 1968, Johnny and June accepted a Grammy Award in Nashville for the best country performance by a duo or group for the song "Jackson."

The next day, March 1, they were married in Franklin, Kentucky. They would make their home at a house on a lake in Hendersonville, Tennessee.

In May 1968, *Johnny Cash at Folsom Prison* hit record stores. The songs on the album were taken from a pair of live performances at Folsom (California)  State Prison earlier that year. "It was the most appreciative audience I've ever seen," June said at the time. "They feel like he belongs to them because of 'Folsom Prison Blues.'"

The album was wildly successful. It spent eighty-nine weeks on *Billboard*'s country chart, including four at number one, and one hundred twenty-two weeks on the pop chart, reaching number thirteen.

Johnny was at the peak of his popularity. In 1969, he had nine albums on the country chart! His song "A Boy Named Sue" reached number two on *Billboard*'s pop chart. One out of every five records sold in the United States that year was by Johnny Cash. And he even had his own weekly television program, *The Johnny Cash Show*. It aired on ABC for three seasons beginning in June 1969.

Johnny Cash performing with singer
Linda Ronstadt on *The Johnny Cash Show*

His personal life was reaching a high point as well. He was happily married to June, and they had a son, John Carter Cash, who was born on March 3, 1970.

Six weeks later, Johnny sang for President Richard Nixon and 250 guests at the White House in Washington, DC. "His music speaks to all America," President Nixon said. "It speaks in stories about Americans that touch the heart of America—north, east, south and west."

Johnny performed some of his best-known songs, like "Folsom Prison Blues" and "Five Feet High and Rising," plus some of his favorite gospel songs. Near the end of the evening, he thanked the president and the first lady for their hospitality. Then he publicly asked the president to help end the Vietnam War. "We pray, Mr. President, that you can end this war in Vietnam

sooner than you hope or think it can be done, and we hope and pray that our boys will be back home and there will soon be peace in our mountains and valleys."

It was a polite, but shocking, way for Johnny to speak out on behalf of the young men who were fighting what many Americans felt was an unjust war.

The Vietnam War

The Vietnam War was a nearly twenty-year war between South Vietnam and North Vietnam that lasted from November 1955 through April 1975. South Vietnam was supported by anti-communist countries such as the United States. North Vietnam was supported by communist countries such as the Soviet Union and China.

The war became increasingly unpopular with Americans as the United States became more and more involved in the 1960s. Television coverage of the war and images in American newspapers and magazines shocked the American public. People wanted to know why the United States was fighting in this war so far from home. Protests erupted in many parts of the country, especially in Washington, DC, and on college campuses.

The direct involvement of the United States in the Vietnam War ended in 1973. By then, more than 58,000 Americans had lost their lives in the fighting. Another 153,000 had been wounded. And many others suffered emotional trauma that would last a lifetime.

CHAPTER 7
The Man in Black

By this time, Johnny was often called the Man in Black. Everyone wanted to know where the nickname came from.

The obvious answer was that Johnny always wore black onstage. He liked it. But there was

more to it than that. Wearing black also became his symbol of rebellion, of fighting against injustice and society's problems. And Johnny put his feelings down in a song released in 1971, "Man in Black."

"I wrote the song because people were asking me why I've worn black, basically ever since I've been in the music business," Johnny said.

In the song, Johnny wrote that he wore black for the "poor and the beaten down," and for the "prisoner who has long paid for his crime." He wore it for the "sick and lonely old" and for people who "never read, or listened to, the words that Jesus said." He wore it for people hooked on drugs and for young men who died in wars. The words came straight from his heart.

"Man in Black" reached number three on *Billboard*'s country chart. The album on which it was included, also called *Man in Black*, rose to number one.

Johnny was in great demand in concert. In 1975, he performed 162 shows, his most ever in a single year. Some of them were as far away as Japan, Austria, and Germany. Always he would sing his most popular songs, such as "Ring of Fire" and "I Walk the Line." He would also include his favorite gospel songs, such as "Peace in the Valley" and "He Turned the Water into Wine," which he wrote himself after a visit to Israel.

June often accompanied Johnny onstage, and Marshall Grant continued to play bass. But guitarist Luther Perkins had died in 1968. Many other musicians spent time with the touring group, including longtime drummer W. S. Holland, guitarist Carl Perkins, and Marty Stuart, who played several instruments.

Then, Johnny liked to say, he "disappeared" in the 1980s. But that wasn't true. He opened the decade by being inducted into the Country Music Hall of Fame in 1980. At forty-eight years old, he was its youngest living inductee.

Midway through the decade, Johnny joined Waylon Jennings, Kris Kristofferson, and Willie Nelson in a group calling themselves the Highwaymen. Country fans loved to see the four longtime superstars, who all seemed to be enjoying themselves, together onstage.

The four legends recorded a number one album in 1985 that was simply called *The Highwaymen*.

The Highwaymen

Johnny was inducted into the Rock and Roll Hall of Fame in 1992. Then, in 1993, the final chapter in Johnny's long music career began.

Johnny Cash performs at his induction into
the Rock and Roll Hall of Fame

That year, he met music producer Rick Rubin, who asked Johnny to join his record company, American Recordings.

Johnny wasn't sure what to think. Rubin was a very successful producer, but he mostly worked

Rick Rubin

with rock and rap artists, not country and gospel. What would younger fans think of a country musician who was over sixty years old? It turned out they thought he was terrific! With the album *American Recordings* in 1994, Johnny gained a new generation of fans. The album featured thirteen songs of just Johnny singing while playing his guitar, most of them recorded in Rubin's living room in Los Angeles or at Johnny's house in Hendersonville, Tennessee.

"My fondest memories are just of hanging out and hearing his stories," Rubin said of Johnny. "He didn't speak much but, if you drew him out, he seemed to know everything. He was shy and quiet but a wise, wise man."

Johnny went on to make three other albums with Rick Rubin. It seemed like from then on, much of his life was filled with awards and honors. In 1996, he was honored by the Kennedy Center, which recognizes performers for their contributions to American culture and character.

President Bill Clinton

"From the heartland of America, he's sung for the people who *are* the heart of America," President Bill Clinton said at the Kennedy Center Honors tribute. "Through his music, he has proved again and again the redeeming power of struggle and faith. And he has made country music not just music for our country but for the entire world."

Johnny was a friend of President Clinton, a fellow Arkansan, as he was with every president

Johnny Cash and President Bill Clinton

since Richard Nixon: Gerald Ford, Jimmy Carter, Ronald Reagan, George H. W. Bush, and George W. Bush.

Johnny's wife, June Carter Cash, died in Nashville, Tennessee, at age seventy-three in May 2003 following heart surgery. Johnny tried to busy himself with work, but his own health was declining. He died of complications from diabetes less than four months later, on September 12, 2003 in Nashville. He was seventy-one.

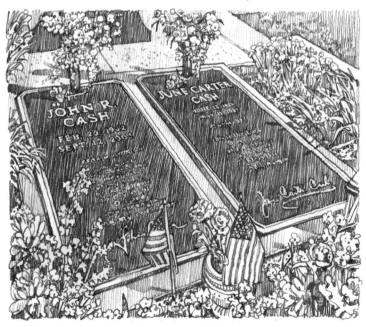

US postage stamp featuring Johnny Cash

The awards and honors continued after Johnny's death. He was inducted into the Gospel Music Hall of Fame in 2011, honored with a US postage stamp in 2013, and inducted into the Grammy Hall of Fame in 2018. In 2019, Arkansas announced it would erect a statue of Johnny to represent the state at the US Capitol in Washington, DC.

Johnny produced an incredible amount of music in his lifetime. He recorded nearly one hundred albums. His work was released in twenty-six countries. He performed thousands of concerts. Although Johnny is mostly remembered as a country singer, he was a

Johnny's album *Johnny Cash* features rockabilly music

versatile performer who appealed to fans of many different music styles, including gospel, folk, blues, and rockabilly.

Johnny used his gift to entertain and befriend both presidents and prisoners. He traveled all over the world, but he always returned to his country roots. He was successful and wealthy, but he wanted to help those who were neither.

"He was willing and able to be the champion of people who didn't have one," said Kris Kristofferson, his friend and fellow member of the Highwaymen.

Perhaps his plaque at the Country Music Hall of Fame in Nashville best sums up who Johnny Cash was.

Kris Kristofferson

It reads, in part: "Songwriter, historian, fighter of causes; friend to the deprived and troubled, friend of great men; a leader in the temporal [earthly] world, and follower in the spiritual world, Johnny Cash is the total entertainer."

Timeline of Johnny Cash's Life

1932 — Born J.R. Cash on February 26 in Kingsland, Arkansas

1950 — Joins the US Air Force as a radio operator

1954 — Marries Vivian Liberto on August 7

1955 — Releases first single for Sun Records, "Hey, Porter," as Johnny Cash

1956 — Appears for the first time on the *Grand Ole Opry* in Nashville, Tennessee, where he meets June Carter

1958 — Signs with Columbia Records

1959 — In Huntsville, Texas, plays a prison concert for the first time

1967 — Marriage to Vivian Liberto ends in divorce

1968 — Marries June Carter on March 1 in Franklin, Kentucky

— Releases landmark album, *Johnny Cash at Folsom Prison*

1969 — *The Johnny Cash Show* debuts on ABC television

1970 — Performs at the White House for President Richard Nixon and guests

1980 — Inducted into the Country Music Hall of Fame

1992 — Inducted into the Rock and Roll Hall of Fame

1994 — Releases his first album, *American Recordings*, with producer Rick Rubin

2003 — Dies in Nashville, Tennessee

Timeline of the World

1932 — Franklin D. Roosevelt is elected president of the United States for the first of a record four times

1941 — The United States enters World War II after its naval station at Pearl Harbor, Hawaii, is attacked

1945 — World War II ends

1947 — Jackie Robinson of the Brooklyn Dodgers becomes the first Black player in the modern era of Major League Baseball

1959 — The first annual Grammy Awards are held to recognize outstanding achievement in the music industry

1963 — President John F. Kennedy is assassinated

1974 — Richard Nixon resigns as president of the United States after the Watergate scandal

1976 — Steve Jobs, Steve Wozniak, and Ronald Wayne start Apple Computer, Inc.

1979 — Sony introduces the Walkman, a portable cassette tape player, to the United States

1981 — Cable television network MTV begins broadcasting music videos

1990 — The Hubble Space Telescope is launched

2001 — On September 11, almost three thousand people are killed in attacks at the World Trade Center in New York City; the Pentagon in Arlington, Virginia; and in rural Shanksville, Pennsylvania

Bibliography

*Books for young readers

Cash, John Carter. *House of Cash: The Legacies of My Father, Johnny Cash*. San Rafael, CA: Insight Editions, 2011.

Cash, Johnny, with Patrick Carr. *Cash: The Autobiography*. San Francisco: HarperSan Francisco, 1997.

Hilburn, Robert. *Johnny Cash: The Life*. New York: Little, Brown and Company, 2013.

Light, Alan. *Johnny Cash: The Life and Legacy of the Man in Black*. Washington, DC: Smithsonian Books, 2018.

*Neri, G. *Hello, I'm Johnny Cash*. Somerville, MA: Candlewick Press, 2014.